# PLETHORA

## MY POETIC EXPEDITION

AF581583

T.S. AKSHAYA

Copyright © T.S. AKSHAYA
All Rights Reserved.

This book has been self-published with all reasonable efforts taken to make the material error-free by the author. No part of this book shall be used, reproduced in any manner whatsoever without written permission from the author, except in the case of brief quotations embodied in critical articles and reviews.

The Author of this book is solely responsible and liable for its content including but not limited to the views, representations, descriptions, statements, information, opinions and references ["Content"]. The Content of this book shall not constitute or be construed or deemed to reflect the opinion or expression of the Publisher or Editor. Neither the Publisher nor Editor endorse or approve the Content of this book or guarantee the reliability, accuracy or completeness of the Content published herein and do not make any representations or warranties of any kind, express or implied, including but not limited to the implied warranties of merchantability, fitness for a particular purpose. The Publisher and Editor shall not be liable whatsoever for any errors, omissions, whether such errors or omissions result from negligence, accident, or any other cause or claims for loss or damages of any kind, including without limitation, indirect or consequential loss or damage arising out of use, inability to use, or about the reliability, accuracy or sufficiency of the information contained in this book.

Made with ♥ on the Notion Press Platform
www.notionpress.com

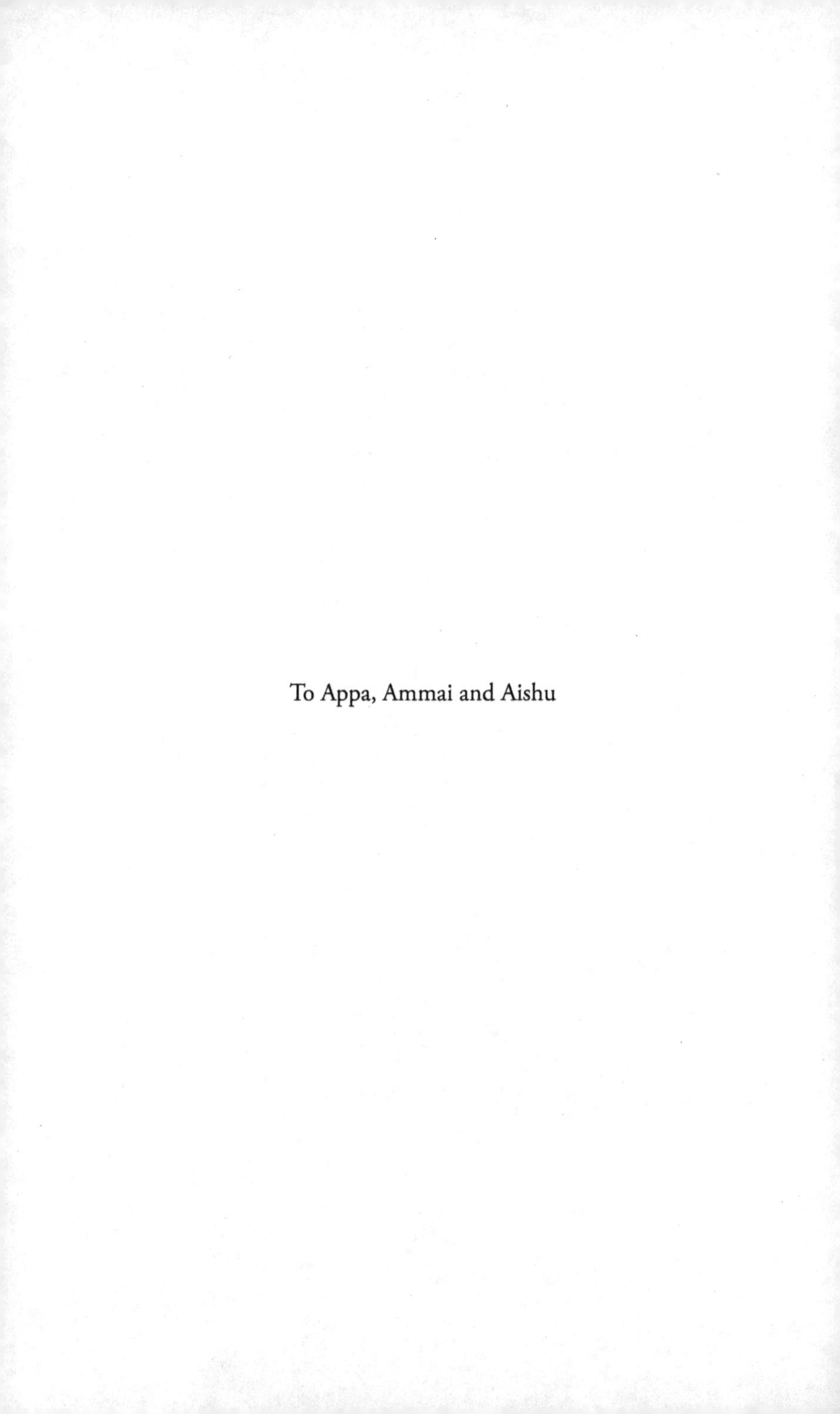

To Appa, Ammai and Aishu

# Contents

# Contents

# Acknowledgements

'Plethora' is the cumulation of a prolonged effort, implemened over the years. It is the outcome of exploring, imagining and reminiscing things and incorporating it into a poetic outline. I would like to extend my sincere gratitude to my parents, for encouraging me to pursue my dreams. Without their support, I wouldn't have been able to discover the captivating world of literature and poetry in particular. I would also like to thank my teachers, for guiding me throughout my literary expedition and motivating me at every step. The poems included in this work have been inspired by different people and I would like to convey my gratitude to all of them as well. I would also like to thank in advance, all the readers for choosing this book. Thank you for your support. Hope you have an amazing reading experience.

# 1. MATHS

Maths is vast,
like an ocean past,
doing Maths
is a very good task.
Maths is full of equations
which has its own solutions,
finding these solutions
is full of variations.
Maths is full of geometry,
And the great trigonometry,
Found out by a genius,
By his work so tedious.
Once you get involved in it,
You will never come back from it,
You will start loving it
and will never stop doing it.
Maths is a very great creation,
And has good tradition,
Numbers are wonders,
As their great splendour.

# 2. QUEST OF LIFE

Commerce is a subject
which makes us smart,
when we master this subject,
we become its part.
It is interesting
if we do not keep resting
and start working
to obtain knowledge cracking.
Once we start liking it,
We can never stop learning it,
We will get involved in it
and start learning more from it.
Economics is the basis
to achieve great success
in the world of commerce,
where there is no leisure.
Business is a test
which requires a lot of zest,
For one to pass this test,
He has to work his best.
Accountancy is a body
of practice and theory,
Recording, communicating,

Is not mere counting.
Life is ongoing
with lending and borrowing,
To lead a happy life,
One must be wise.

# 3. LIFE

Birth is a miracle
which brings us to this world,
It is a spectacle
that prospers the world.
Childhood is a stage
of magic and joy,
But teenage is rage
with anger and ploy.
Maturity, the essence
that cures this rage,
Leads to the presence
of the adult stage.
Adulthood, the phase
of rush and rage,
Is quite a race
to the final stage.
Old age, the pace
declines but stays,
Fear, ablaze,
Death the final stage.
Life is a game
of time and space,
Survival the prize,

Death, a final grace.

# 4. MY SOULKEEPER'S MOTHER

My soul keeper's mother
is a victim of life,
But she is a fighter,
Who transformed her life.
She is invincible
like a fierce tide,
Overcoming obstacles
with a huge smile.
The epitome of motherhood,
Caring and kind,
She is a role model
for every kind.
A survivor is she
in the battle of life,
Protecting her family
from every cry.
Elegance is an attribute,
Fitting for herself,
Love and compassion,
Defining her self.
My soul keeper's mother
is a strong woman,

Who deserves admiration
from each and everyone.
She is an inspiration
for every soul,
Family is her vision,
Its unity, her goal.
Poetry and photography
are her twin passions,
Cooking for her family,
Yet another rendition.
A pillar of strength
for her dear children,
She's the perfect partner
for her caring husband.
Life was not easy
during early years,
But with love and care
she overcame her fears.
My soul keeper's mother
is an extraordinary being,
Caring for her family
is her pivotal dealing.

# 5. LONELINESS

Loneliness is a feeling
which has no healing
or great consoling
by any fellow being.
It is a mental state
of rejection and hate
from within the mind
saying no one is kind.
Ignorance is bliss
but not in this case
for we are considered
like no one in ways.
Don't be sad
because we are all lonely,
Worldly relations
are just God's folly.
Loneliness is an expression
that makes us sad,
To overcome this emotion
we must try hard.

# 6. THE OLD HARDWARE STORE (1)

The ancient smell wafting
from the old hardware store,
Evoking memories
from my childhood days.
Visiting the store,
After daily chores,
An ethereal feeling
with people I adore.
A magical abode
to the child's sight,
Filled with small surprises
like a wonderland.
Adulthood wiped-out
all the childhood wonder
from my mind
Why? I ponder.
Oh! How I wish my sight
of childhood restored,
Will make the hardware store,
An unbounded sight.

# 7. X-RAY OF MY LOVER'S MIND

Oh! How I wish we had
the feeling of true, mutual love,
Serene and calming
and not always a ploy.
He is engrossed
in the famous play,
'Romeo and Juliet',
Oh! What a day.
He was my Romeo
until that day
when he aloud proclaimed
that my love was a game.
My mind shattered
into a million pieces,
Overcome with anger
I ran across places.
I felt betrayed
but not ashamed,
my love was true and sane
yet he couldn't return.
He was my life
and my guiding light,

but his thoughts and talks,
proved me wrong and right.
Love is a puzzling feel
of what we think is real,
that's not always the case,
although sometimes it stays.
His mind was naive,
innocent and sweet,
but the x-ray received,
showed it wasn't so right.
My love was so blind,
but my sight (inner) alert and bright,
Rendering visions
of my lover's mind.
The x-ray of his mind,
Cleared the mist covering my mind,
Soothing and cleaning
the whole of my mind.

# 8. CRAZY PSYCHE

What a crazy psyche
the lady has,
rare, unique,
she might surpass that.
Her ideas are strange
for our mental range,
some might find it sane,
but, most say "INSANE"!
Normalcy is a state
that doesn't exist
in her unique world,
with her crazy psyche.
Observant and sly,
she is not shy,
eavesdropping an act,
performed by her tact.
"Extra" is a way
by which she describes
other people's lives
with her little lies.
The grey, short woman
is not always kind,
but she is not cruel

to the mankind.
She's not evil,
just a bit sly,
ignorance occupies
her soul a tiny bit.
What a crazy psyche
the lady has,
rare, unique,
she might surpass that.

# 9. PARTLY-WASHED COFFEE CUPS

Coffee is a beverage
consumed by many,
but, partly-washed coffee cups
is not a routine.
R___, a lifesaver,
she must feel pity
for the drops of heaven
in those coffee cups.
Rescuing the contents
of those unclean mugs,
definitely her decision
by partly-washing them.
Maybe its an error
from her sneaky side,
or an act of pleasure,
intentional and blind.
Partly-washing coffee cups,
yes, a daily chore,
saving them tiny drops
of tasty brew.

# 10. PHONE-TASTIC

Her life is phone-tastic,
videos and songs,
news stories and graphics,
keep her all engrossed.
Phone is the oxygen
to her very soul,
all her ambitions,
ready to be torn.
Architecture was her dream,
long before exposed
to the world of phones
where she's all alone.
Headphones are the only
ornament she wears,
long, wiry,
she loves it there.
The sound of blazing music,
entering her mind,
disturbing the calmness
of the inner mind.
But, Ai___ doesn't care,
for she's become a prey
of this vicious system

which leads her astray.
Perhaps clear vision,
can break this negative bond,
and motivate her mission
of her dream job.
Her life is phone-tastic,
videos and songs,
news stories and graphics
keep her all engrossed.

# 11. DEFINING PATRIOTISM

Love for one's own country
is the meaning of this term,
hard work and compassion
to make the nation great.
Proud of our country
we can always be,
when we do the needful
for its well-being.
Maintaining the culture
of the native land
is never a torture
when we understand.
Supporting the homeland's
developmental hike,
and curbing its downfall
should be done alike.
Feeling patriotic
is a natural trait
when we love the country
and are proud of its state.
Patriotism an emotion
of ardent faith,

dedication and devotion
to that homely place.
Love for one's own country
is the meaning of this term,
hard work and compassion
to make the nation great.

# 12. CANOPY OF NATURE

Canopy of nature,
abundant yet wild,
a never-ending cycle
of life design.
Dense forest, jungles,
ruggedly terrains,
smooth flowing water,
valleys and plains.
Creatures big or small,
all staying there,
Co- existing merrily
in heat and rain.
Epitome of creation,
nature is kind,
but, it emits fury
when we always deny.
Preserving this treasure
should be our goal,
attaining some pleasure
will happen on its own.
Mother nature provides
life's crude form,

moulding it fine,
existence defines.
Experimenting elements
of nature's domain,
rejuvenates the feeling
of our mental train.
Canopy of nature,
wholesome yet drained
at certain places
like desert trails.

# 13. COLOURS OF MY LIFE

"Its over", he said,
my face engulfed pallor,
drained of all the hues,
I stood there helpless.
Words crafted sweetly
made me blush,
constantly rosy,
countenance pretty.
A tinge of irony
embedded in life,
satirical hues
spreading through the sky.
Dancing in front of my eyes
his blue, linen shirt
met with the sky,
scattered yet bonded.
His eyes were pale,
ocean blue,
beautiful, caring,
deep- expressive.
Protecting me
lovingly he said,

The man of my life,
"Come on sweetheart, let's go".
My daddy held my hand,
an energy surpassed,
all His memories,
disappeared: like grey smoke.

# 14. A FUNNY TAKE ON 'LOVE'

"What is love?" I ask,
Bewildered. Clueless.
Is it a formula
or some calculation;
A tasty recipe of
accurate proportions?
Or a soulful song,
'movie adaptation';
It is a sensation,
a charming occasion!

# 15. I STILL REMEMBER THE DAY

I still remember the day
she passed through that hallway,
smiling my way
to make a good day.
A green shawl waved
from the window pane,
fluttering away
where my heart lay.
The girl came near
without any fear
and shook my hand
like someone too dear.
I still remember the day
we talked without a pause,
enjoying each moment
as it came to a close.
The air filled with friendship
suffocated us both,
our bond grew stronger
and stronger we strove.

She started loving my voice
or so I thought,
since I talk all day
yet, she doesn't complain.
I still remember the day
she gave me strength
and stood by my side
when all others left.
My true, faithful friend!

# 16. LOVE FOR ETERNITY

A burning kiss he gave,
passionate and strong,
heat waves running
all throughout my veins.
His powerful gaze
sweeps me off my feet,
radiating goodness,
can't live without him.
Our moments together
are intense and deep,
my whole body trembles
when he touches me.
Life without his presence
is impossible,
removing darkness,
enlightening souls.
Sunshine the saviour,
people worship him,
existence eternal,
universe not dim.

# 17. SOUL COMPANIONS

Resting in my hands,
moving with the wind,
a sweet fragrance
fills up to the brim.
Nurturing it
is my favourite thing,
spending time with it,
Utter bliss!
Takes me to a world,
an utopian dream,
magic and fantasy
floating like clouds.
Oh how I wish
I were a character
of the famous book
that's "Harry Potter".
Dragons, owls, spells,
houses, cloaks and halls,
Hogwarts mystical,
unique yet mundane.
Books make me whole
capturing my soul,

without these jewels,
I think I will choke.

# 18. THE SACRED BRONZE RIDDLE

The sacred bronze riddle
God bequeathed them,
used by holy figures,
possesses mystical powers.
A glorious light emerges
from its spout so bright,
this divine radiance
has blinded my sight.
In the sturdy vessel,
dark potions brew,
emitting hissing noises,
hated by a few.
Belonged to forefathers,
preserved throughout life,
Alas time has come
for me to get that prize.
But I'm unwilling,
confused and anxious,
owning such a thing
is not my true calling.

# 19. WISHES OF THE HEART

An unknown visitor
knocked on the door,
amidst a pile of snow
he shivered and frowned.
When she opened the door
and greeted him more,
words escaped his thoughts
replaced by new found love.
On a snowy night,
dreaming of fair delight,
enchanted by that sight
A_____ let out a sigh.
She was very pretty
with an exquisite smile,
Oh it is a pity
that he couldn't say 'Hi'.
Days were spent regardless
preparing for small talk,
but everything subsided
at that confused glance.
Unaware of all this
she moved on in life,

got married and had kids,
even bought a house.
Knowing the truth about her,
sadness welled up in his heart,
soon it just disappeared
along with the past.
Occupying the picture frame
he gazed at her divine face,
hoping he was with her
like a real pair.

# 20. TRAPPED

The green ottoman
underneath the chair,
graced by her feet
was not something rare.
She only sat there
on days that were bare
like a sole mare,
with no one to care.
Tears blurring her vision,
wiping away dreams,
ambitions lay forgotten ,
buried elsewhere.
Spirited cries of victory
became happy memories,
freedom beyond her grasp
felt far away.
A burning stench
woke her up
ending the reverie
of loss and misery.

# 21. BOREDOM

Hated by the mass,
sometime found in class,
can cause chaos,
even physical brawls.
Its arrival unexpected,
departure unnoticed,
free from any bias,
has different levels.
Money or social status
is not a concern,
boredom can hit anyone
and take turns.
An opportunity, a problem,
it is a lot of things,
time is of the essence,
forcing us to think.
Cure for it a plenty,
the answer is the root,
will disappear quickly,
once that is removed.

# 22. SEPARATION

They were one
held in an embrace,
but as times changed
parted ways.
Hatred grew,
corrupting their souls,
attacking the other,
soon became a chore
Memories forever,
the love was always true,
yet, vengeance gained power,
destroying old and new.
Separation is painful
and hurts the soul,
piercing cruelly
like a mighty sword.

# 23. IDENTITY

Identity is not just a name,
or a little fame,
it is a culture
of wide acclaim.
His identity remains unknown,
even though he looks
through the glass window,
almost every day.
Who is he?
my mind wandered,
curious to know his
IDENTITY.
He looked at me
through the window,
sometimes smiled,
sometimes waved.
Was it a smile?
now, I ponder,
or a frown
of hate and anger.
I will never know.

# 24. TWILIGHT

A young enchanting maiden
clad in saffron robes,
little specks of purple
gleaming like jewels.
Her knight in shining armour
awaiting his lover's call,
an angel sent from heaven,
beautiful, divine.
Deep in the woods
impatiently he waits
for twilight
to reach his gaze.
Soon she came,
glowing, deeply in love,
illuminating the surroundings
with a pretty smile.
Darkness filled the atmosphere
when she heard the news
and fled,
Tears a few.
Twilight was distressed,
never left her room
till the next evening

with energy restored.
She loved her people,
subjects of Araca,
seeing their happy faces
became jubilant and gay.
Twilight was cheerful again.

# 25. LABYRINTH OF LIES

An eternity has passed
since I entered the Lair
of deception and hatred,
orchestrated by the Liar.
Unaware of the year,
I tied up my hair,
ready to meet the Liar
and begin our game.
I was just a puppet,
controlled by the puppeteer,
my mind filled with fear
as I entered his lair.
His intentions were pretty clear
and he didn't seem to care
of me and my "petty fear",
Just gave me a stare.
Years passed quickly,
so did his games,
yet he held on to me
with nothing to spare.
The labyrinth of lies
looks like a cosy chamber,

but once you enter,
it will become clear...

www.ingramcontent.com/pod-product-compliance
Lightning Source LLC
LaVergne TN
LVHW040926150826
845672LV00007B/2228

*9798891332546*